Step into the world of your imagination
as you colour

COLOUR ME

relax Kids

Step into the world of your imagination
as you colour

Marneta Viegas

OUR STREET
BOOKS

Winchester, UK
Washington, USA

JOHN HUNT PUBLISHING

First published by Our Street Books, 2021
Our Street Books is an imprint of John Hunt Publishing Ltd., Laurel House,
Station Approach,
Alresford, Hants, SO24 9JH, UK
office@jhpbooks.net
www.johnhuntpublishing.com
www.ourstreet-books.com

For distributor details and how to order please visit the 'Ordering' section on
our website.

ISBN: 978 1 78904 985 5
Library of Congress Control Number: 2021942562

A CIP catalogue record for this book is available from the British Library.

Design: Amber Sutton
Illustrations: Frankie Taylor

Printed by: Gutenberg Press Ltd - Gudja Road, Tarxien GXQ 2902 Malta

We operate a distinctive and ethical publishing philosophy in
all areas of our business, from our global network of authors to
production and worldwide distribution.

THE MAGIC PAINT BRUSH

Close your eyes and imagine you have a Magic Paint Brush.
What words and pictures would you like to draw
with this Magic Paintbrush?

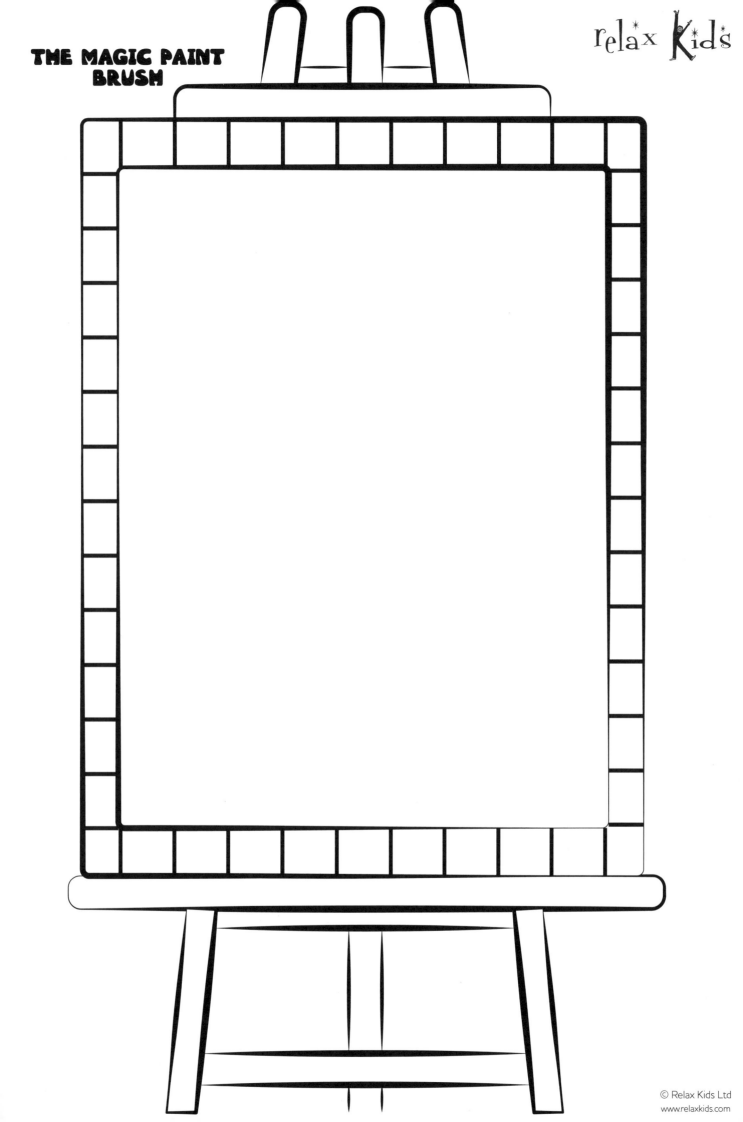

THE MAGIC BOX

Close your eyes and imagine you have a Magic Box.

THE MAGIC BOX

relax Kids

Draw what you see in your
Magic Box

© Relax Kids Ltd
www.relaxkids.com

GRATITUDE NOTES

Write down all the things you are thankful for.

SPECIAL MESSAGES

Who would you like to send a special message to?
Write your special messages on these postcards and decorate them.

ENERGY BOOST

Close your eyes and take in a deep breath. Imagine you are filling with energy. How does this energy boost feel?
Can you draw the feeling?

HAPPY PLACE

Close your eyes and imagine you are in your happy place.
Draw your happy place. You could even try drawing with your eyes still
closed. Whenever you want to go back to your happy place, imagine
you are flicking a switch and take yourself there.

TIME TRAVEL MACHINE

Close your eyes and imagine you are in a Time Travel Machine.
Go back or forward in time and draw what you see in your
imagination.

TIME TRAVEL MACHINE

WONDERFUL YOU

Close your eyes and think about all the wonderful
things about you. Draw and write down all the things
that make you special and wonderful.
See if you can hold onto this wonderful feeling.

Close your eyes and imagine you are a Superhero with superhero powers. Choose colours to represent your powers.
Draw yourself as a Superhero with your superhero powers.

POWER:
FLYING

POWER:
INVISIBILITY

POWER:
STRENGTH

POWER:
TELEPATHY

POWER:
SPEED

POWER:
IMMORTALITY

BRAIN FOOD

What positive words and feelings would you like to fill your brain
with? What colours would you like to fill your mind with?
Fill your brain with good thoughts and feelings.

WORRY TREE

Write all your worries on the leaves of the Worry Tree.

GOLDEN HEART

Fill your Golden Heart with all the good things you have in your life.

HEALTH DRINK

Close your eyes and imagine you have a Health Drink.
Draw pictures of all the healthy ingredients that
are in your Health Drink.

WORRY BALLOONS

Close your eyes and put your worries in your Worry Balloons.
Write them on the Worry Balloons and colour them in.

SECRET DOOR

Close your eyes and imagine you are standing outside a Secret Door.
Draw the amazing things that are waiting for you behind the
Secret Door.

CLOAK OF PROTECTION

Close your eyes and imagine you have a Cloak of Protection.
Colour in your Cloak of Protection.

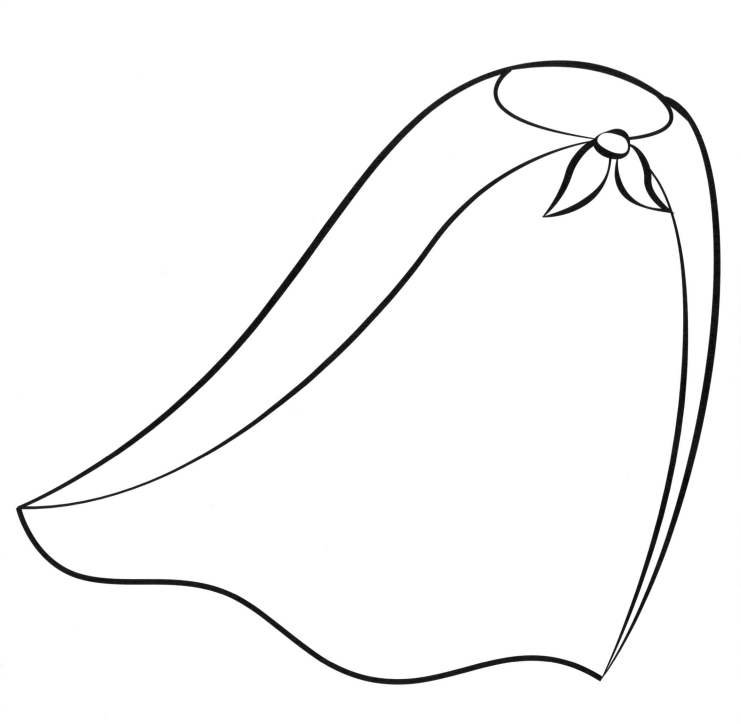

HOT AIR BALLOON

Close your eyes and imagine you are floating up in a Hot Air Balloon.
Draw what you can see from your Hot Air Balloon.

WISHING WELL

Close your eyes and imagine you are throwing a penny in the Wishing Well. You can have 3 wishes.
Fill your thought bubbles with your 3 wishes.

MAGIC WAND

Close your eyes and imagine you have a Magic Wand.
Draw what you would like to come true if you waved your
Magic Wand.

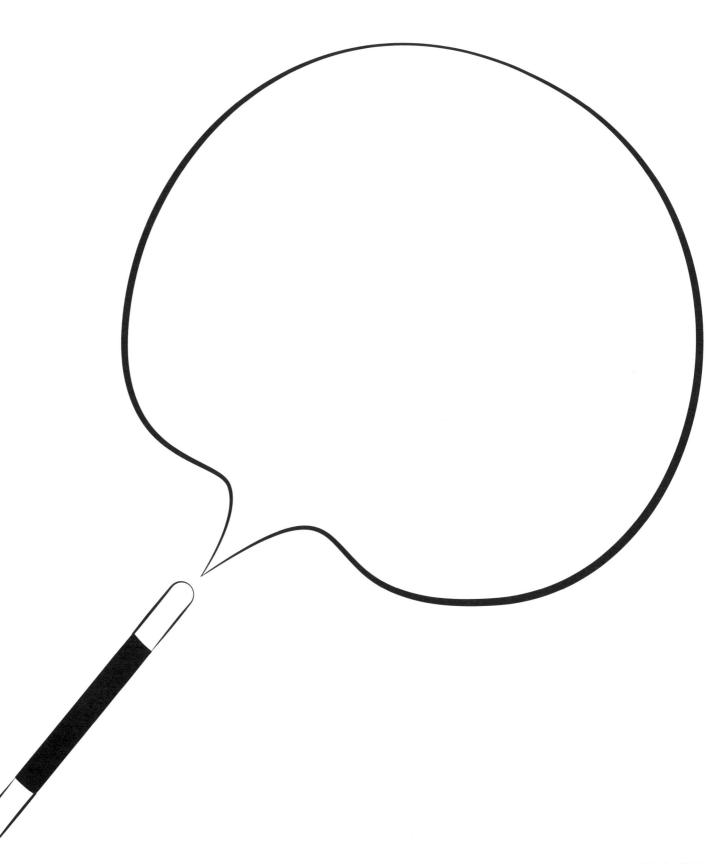

RELAXOMETER

What things make you feel stressed and what things help you feel relaxed? Draw them next to your Relaxometer.

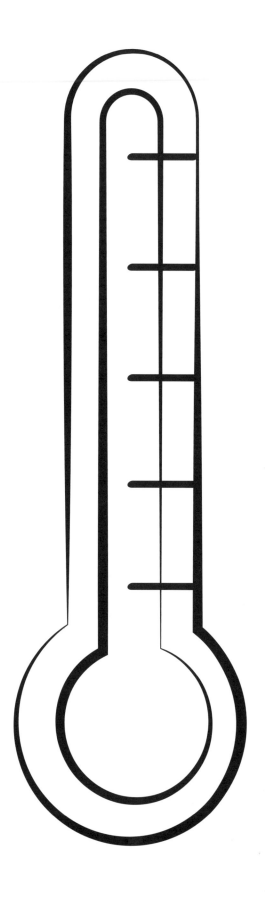

RADIO

Close your eyes and imagine you are listening to some music on the Radio. What does it sound like? How does it make you feel? See if you can draw the sounds and feelings using your colours.

MAGIC CASTLE

Close your eyes and imagine you are in a Magic Castle of Creativity.
You can create whatever you wish.
Draw whatever you would like in your Magic Castle.

POSITIVE PLACE

Close your eyes and take yourself to a positive place.
Draw your Positive Place on this page.

MAGICAL RAINBOW

Close your eyes and imagine you can see a Magical Rainbow.
Draw what you can see at the end of your Rainbow.

CRYSTAL BALL

Close your eyes and imagine yourself in 10 or 20 years time.
Draw what you would like your future to be.

MAGIC CARPET

Close your eyes and imagine you have a Magic Carpet.
Draw where you would like to go on your Magic Carpet.

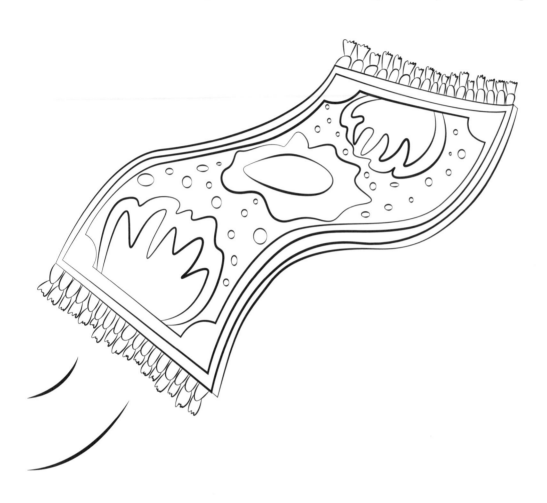

MAGIC LAMP

Write your 3 wishes.

MAGICAL MAZE

Create a colourful maze and find your way to the centre.

Start

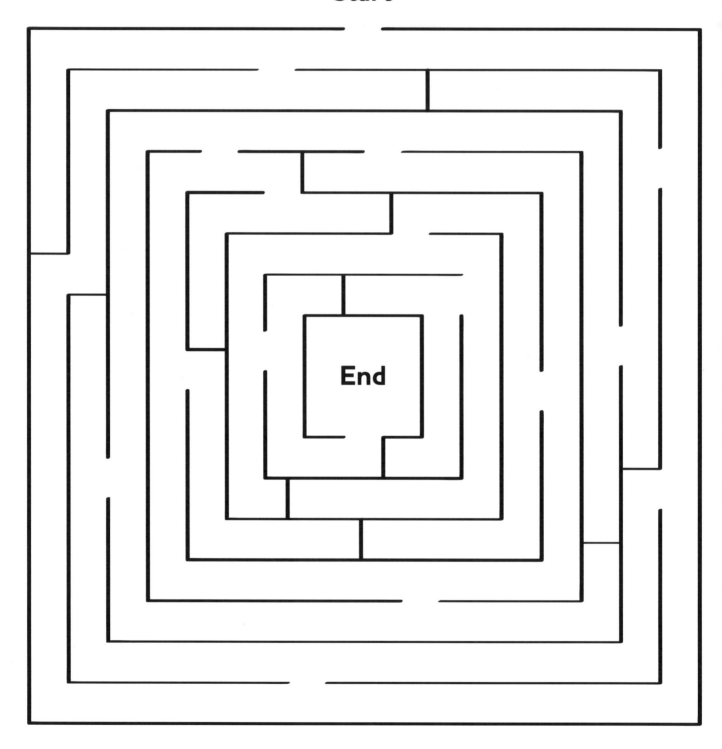

End

PRECIOUS POLAROIDS

Draw what is most precious to you in the polaroids below.

CUP OF JOY

Close your eyes and imagine you are holding a cup of
joy in your hands. Your cup of joy is filled with all the things that make
you feel happy and joyful. What is in your cup of joy?

PICNIC HAMPER

Close your eyes and imagine you are going on a picnic.
Draw what you would take on your picnic in the hamper below.
Who would you go on a picnic with?

MY MONSTER

Imagine a crazy scientist has created a monster for you.
What would your monster look like?

MY MONSTER

relax Kids

NEWSPAPER

Create your own positive newspaper cover

STORY BUNTING

Write a short story in the bunting below.

Once upon a time

the end.

MY CITY

Imagine you can create your own city.
Expand this house into your perfect city/town.

CAVE OF CALM

Draw what's inside your cave of calm.

PEACE BUBBLES

Close your eyes and imagine you are blowing bubbles of peace, love and happiness into the room. Notice how it feels. Colour in your bubbles of peace, love and happiness.

PEACE BUBBLES

relax Kid

© Relax Kid
www.relaxkids

BATH OF WARMTH

Close your eyes and imagine you are lying in a warm bath of bubbles. Draw yourself in your bath of warmth covered in a million bubbles.

BOX OF LOVE

Close your eyes and imagine you are holding a box of love.
What is inside your box of love. Draw all the things you love.

PANTS OF PEACE

Close your eyes and imagine you are wearing your pants of peace. What do they look like? How do they feel?

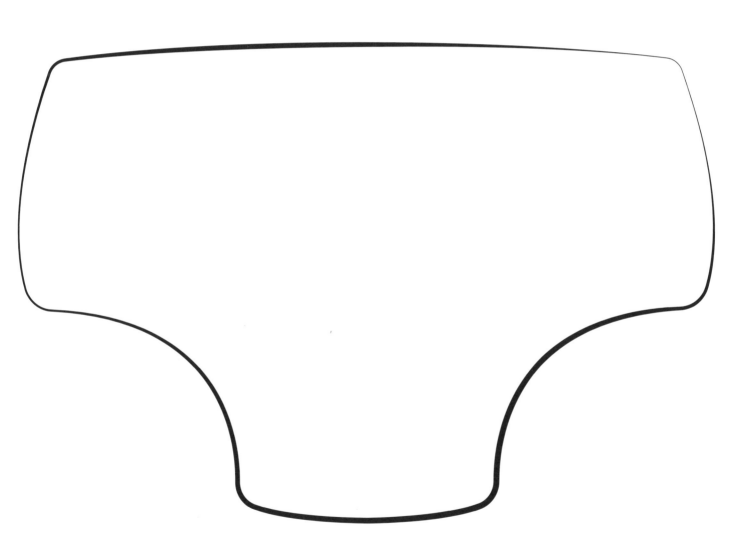

WORLD OF IMAGINATION

Close your eyes and step into the world of your imagination.
What do you see? Draw what you see.

BOTTLE OF COURAGE

Close your eyes and imagine you have a bottle of courage.
This bottle makes you feel courageous and brave.
Colour your bottle of courage.

CIRCLE OF FRIENDSHIP

Close your eyes and imagine you are standing in a circle with all your friends. Draw your friendship circle.

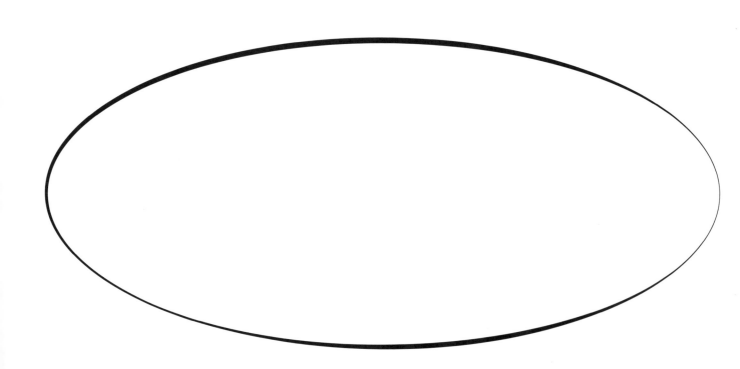

HAT OF COMPLIMENTS

Close your eyes and imagine you are wearing your hat of compliments. Colour in your hat and fill it with compliments and lovely things about yourself.

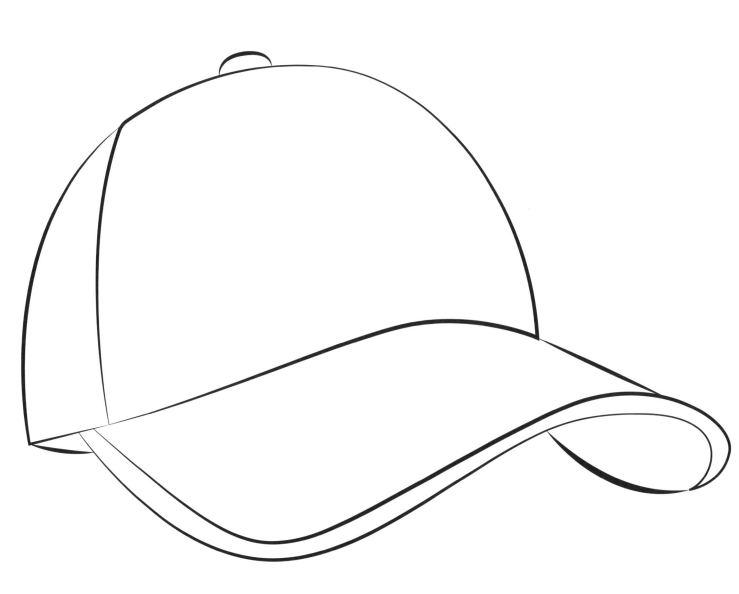

SHOES OF CONFIDENCE

Close your eyes and imagine you have lots of shoes.
You have shoes of peace, shoes of love, shoes of
confidence and shoes of happiness.
Colour in all your shoes and put them on when you need them.

GLASSES OF GREATNESS

Close your eyes and imagine you are wearing your glasses of greatness. These help you feel brave, confident and great. Colour in your glasses of greatness.

PEBBLE OF STILLNESS

Close your eyes and imagine you are on a beach of pebbles.
Choose a pebble and hold it in your hand.
Hold onto your pebble and feel still and peaceful.

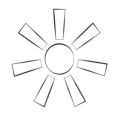

SUN OF RADIANCE

Close your eyes and imagine you are standing under the sun of radiance. It is making you feel so strong and healthy. Draw the rays of the sun.

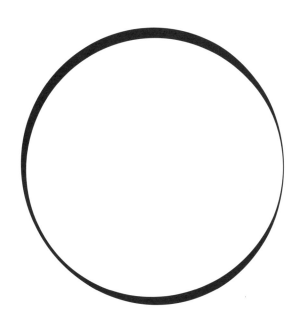

CLOUD OF CALM

Close your eyes and imagine you are lying on your very own cloud of calm. Draw yourself floating on your cloud of calm or write how you feel. Draw what you can see from your cloud of calm.

MAGNET OF ATTRACTION

Close your eyes and imagine your mind is a magnet of attraction. Every time you have a positive thought, your magnet attracts more positivity towards you and you start to feel more and more positive and happy. Draw or write all the things that make you feel happy, confident and peaceful and imagine your magnet attracting good feelings towards you.

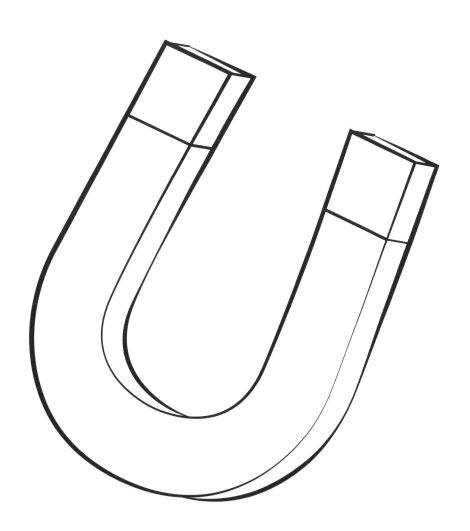

LETTER OF POSITIVITY

Close your eyes and imagine you are writing a letter of positivity.
It is full of lovely things. Write your letter of positivity.

BRIGHT IDEAS

Write down all your amazing ideas

SPECIAL PORTRAITS

Draw the people most special to you.

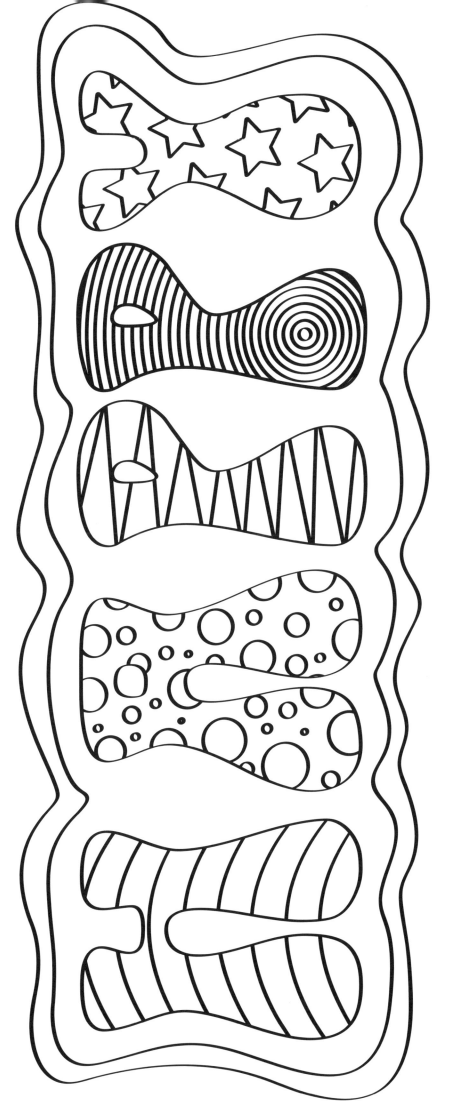

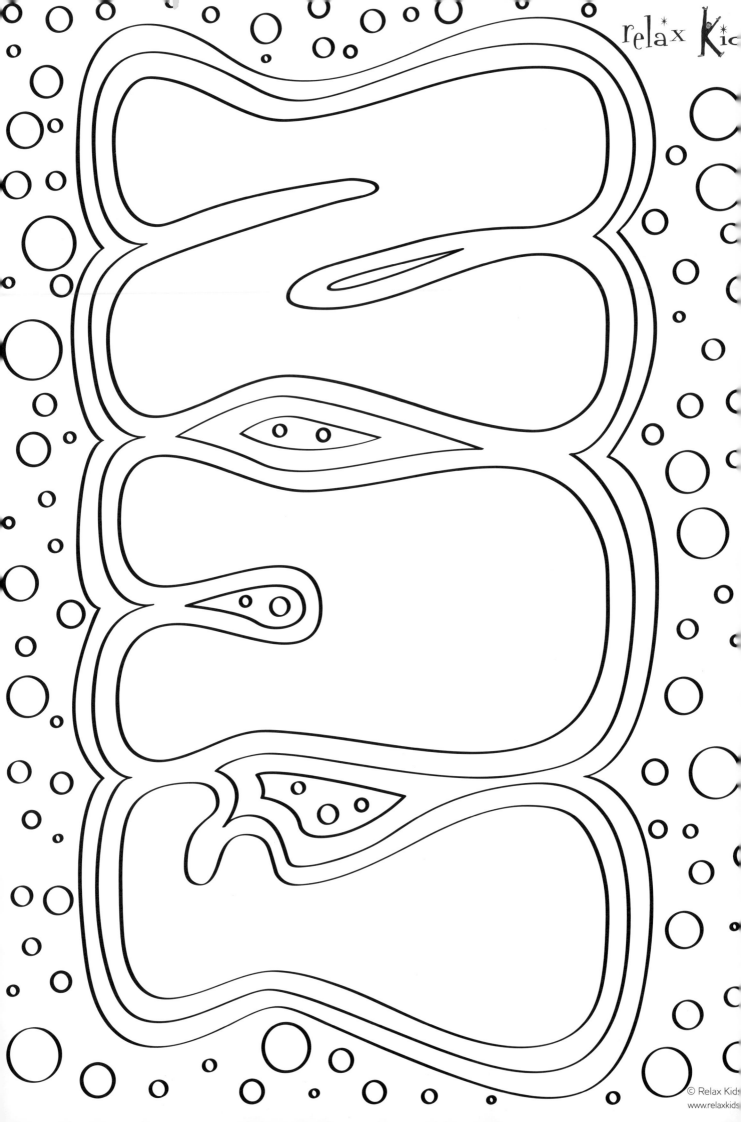

MY ROSETTE

Design yourself your own special rosette. What award would you give yourself?

CELEBRATION CAKE

Imagine you are having a celebration and have to make a special cake.
What are you celebrating? What does your cake look like?

RELAXING BATH

relax Kids

Imagine yourself in this relaxing bath and draw things that calm you down in the bubbles.

FEATHER OF MINDFULNESS

Imagine you have a Feather of Mindfulness, As you colour in your feather, become aware of your thoughts and surroundings. How do you feel?

MY MAGIC HAT

Imagine you have a magical hat and can pull whatever you like from it. What does your magical hat look like? What would you pull out from your magic hat?

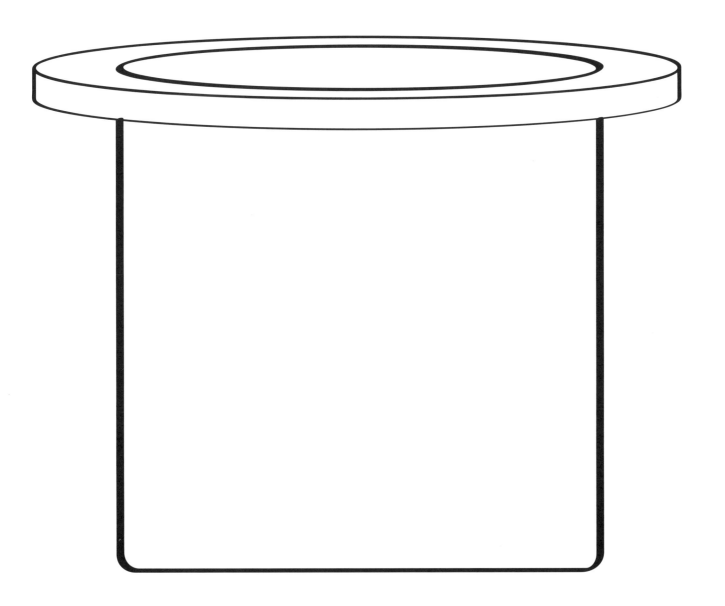

MY FAVOURITE FOOD

Imagine you have a plate of your favourite food infront of you.
How do you feel? What makes this food your favourite?
Draw on the plate below what your favourite food is.

MY GRATITUDE JAR

Imagine you have a Gratitude Jar. Draw in the Jar below all the things you are thankful for.

MAGIC CAULDRON

Imagine you have a magic cauldron and you can make magical potions that will give you anything you desire. What potions would you make in your magic cauldron?

POSITIVITY ALPHABET

Can you think of a positive word for each letter of the alphabet?

A_____ B_____ C_____ D_____

E_____ F_____ G_____ H_____

I_____ J_____ K_____ L_____

M_____ N_____ O_____ P_____

Q_____ R_____ S_____ T_____

U_____ V_____ W_____ X_____

Y_____ Z_____

SLEEPY SLOTH

Imagine you are relaxed like a sleepy Sloth. Colour in the Sloth below thinking about all the things that help you feel relaxed or help you go to sleep.

FEELINGS FORECAST

relax Kids

Imagine your feelings are like the weather and draw
how you feel each day of the week in the boxes.
For example, if you feel sad one day, you might draw rain
clouds and if you were happy you might draw sunshine.

MONDAY

TUESDAY

WEDNESDAY

THURSDAY

FRIDAY

SATURDAY

SUNDAY

AMAZING
ASTRONAUT

Imagine you are an amazing Astronaut travelling through outerspace.
How do you feel? Draw your face in the Astronaut's space helmet.

MY PLANET

Imagine you have discovered a new planet. What would it look like?
Are there any creatures?

MY HEART BEAT

When calm, your heart beat is slow and steady, and when you're excited or nervous, your heart beats quicker. What do you think your heart beat looks like when you're happy or angry?

Calm

Nervous

Angry

Happy

ENORMOUS EMOTIONS

Draw the emotions on the children below.

Angry

Happy

Excited

Nervous

Moody

Bored

Tired

Brave

Shy

WISHING STAR

Imagine you are watching the stars and you see the biggest wishing star shining bright. As you colour in the night sky write in your wishing star what you would wish for.

UNDER THE SEA relax Kids

Imagine you are a mermaid/merman living peacefully under the sea.
How do you feel? What powers do you have? What can you see?
Complete the drawing below.

PERFECT PUMPKIN

Imagine you have a perfect pumpkin which you can carve any picture of expression into it. This is a magical pumpkin so whatever you chose to carve will come true. If you draw a happy face, you will feel happy. What will you carve on your perfect pumpkin?

INTO THE WOODS

Imagine you are travelling into the woods. What do you hear? What can you see? What can you smell? Expand the woods below.

Imagine you have planted a special seed that has grown into the most amazing plant or flower. Draw below what your plant looks like. How do you feel drawing your fabulous flower?

POSITIVE PETALS

Write in the petals of the Sunflower below all the positive qualities about yourself. When you are feeling down, look at your Sunflower to remind yourself how incredible you are.

LLAMA OF LAUGHTER

Imagine you have a pet Llama that laughs
and brings happiness wherever you go. Colour in
your Llama thinking about all the things that make
you laugh or feel happy.

BRILLIANT BOUNCY CASTLE

Imagine you have a brilliant bouncy castle. Draw yourself on your bouncy castle. Where is the bouncy castle? Who are you with? How do you feel?

MY MIND CINEMA

Imagine your at the cinema and can watch back a favoruite memory.
Draw what you can see. How do you feel?

relax Kids

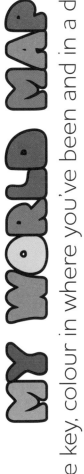

MY WORLD MAP

Using the key, colour in where you've been and in a different colour, colour in where you would like to go.

Where I've Been

Where I'd Like to Go

MARYELLOUS MASKS

Decorate these marvellous masks. Where would you wear them?
How do you feel wearing your masks?

SUPERHERO

Imagine you are a superhero flying over the city.
What powers do you have? How do you feel?
Draw yourself as a superhero.

MY CAMPING ADVENTURE

Imagine you are camping in the great outdoors. Who are you with? What can you see? What can you smell? What can you hear? Draw yourself camping.

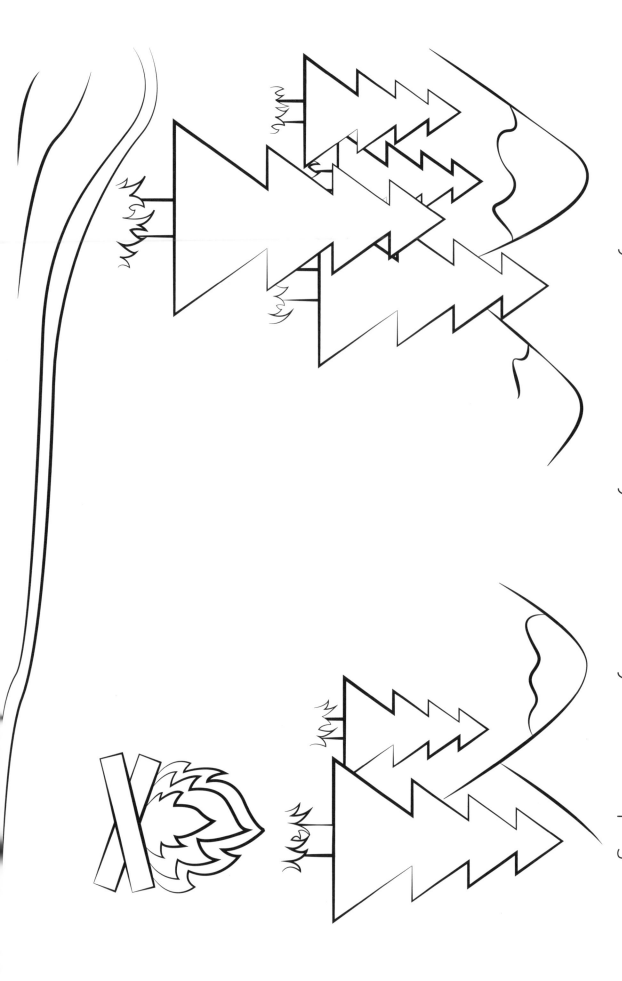

TEEPEE OF DREAMS

Imagine you are going to stay in a Teepee. Who would you stay with?
Where would you stay? What would you dream about?

CALMASAURUS

Imagine you have a Calmasaurus Dinosaur that helps you feelcalm when you are feeling stressed. Draw below what your Calmasaurus looks like.

MY WASHING LINE

Imagine you have a washing line and you can peg out all the things that make you feel happy. special or confident. What is hanging from your washing line?

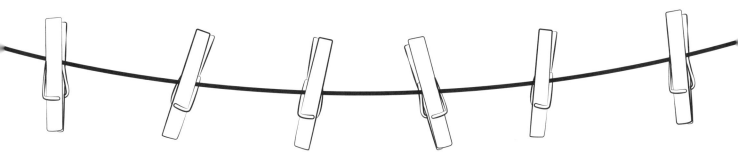

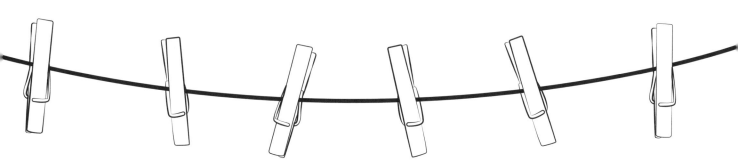

MY COMIC BOOK

Create a story for this superhero, what are their powers?
Who do they save? Do they have an arch enemy?

My super power is...

My name is...

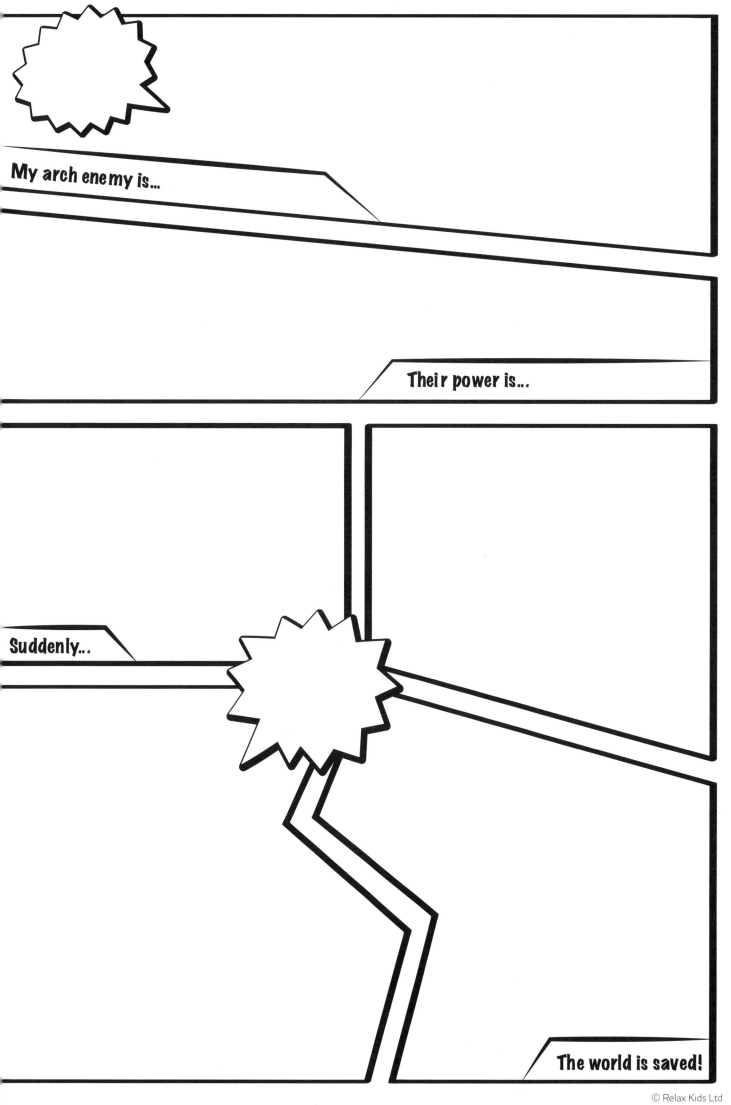

COLOUR BY NUMBERS

Mindfully colour the pictures below using the number chart.
Think about how you feel as you colour.

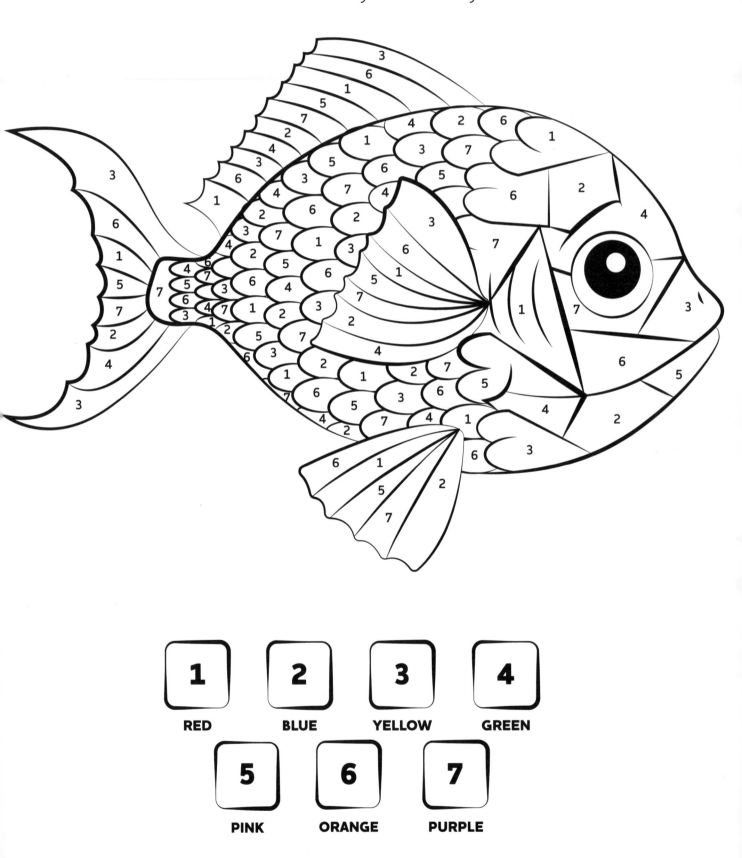

1	**2**	**3**	**4**
RED	BLUE	YELLOW	GREEN

5	**6**	**7**
PINK	ORANGE	PURPLE

1 PURPLE 2 YELLOW 3 BLUE 4 DARK BLUE 5 DARK PURPLE
6 GREEN 7 DARK GREEN 8 PINK 9 DARK PINK 10 ORANGE

© Relax Kids Ltd
www.relaxkids.com

CALM

Relax Kids

© Relax Kids Ltd

www.relaxkids.com

© Relax Kids Ltd

RELAX KIDS PRODUCTS

A selection of mindfulness and affirmation tools suitable for all ages.

AUDIOS

BOOKS

relax Kids

AFFIRMATION CARDS

DOWNLOAD PACKS

AVAILABLE NOW AT:
www.relaxkids.com

TEACH MINDFULNESS TO CHILDREN

Unlock the doors to their imagination.

Become a key person in helping children emotionally regulate, build resilience and learn self-care tools to help them manage life.

relax kids
ONLINE TRAINING
DELIVERED DIRECT TO **YOUR** DOOR
www.relaxkids.com

The Relax Kids 7 step system of relaxation is unique and enjoyable for children of all ages.

Sessions include:
Movement and games
Stretching and breathing exercises
Massage and affirmation games
Relaxation techniques

As a Relax Kids Coach you will receive:

• Training manual • Advertising on the Relax Kids website
• Online resources full of everything you need to run your class
• Access to online chat with other Relax Kids coaches
• Opportunity to run Little Stars, Chill Skills classes, relaxation classes for adults and introductions for schools

BOOK NOW WITH INSTANT ACCESS WITH OUR ONLINE TRAINING OR JOIN US ON ONE OF OUR TRAINING DATES

For more information on our training courses or how to become a Relax Kids coach please visit **www.relaxkids.com** or email **training@relaxkids.com** to recieve an information pack.

Calmaclass gives teachers a toolkit of quick and simple mindful relaxation exercises that can be used at key times of the day. Help support the mental and emotional wellbeing of your pupils with a simple and easy to follow method that requires no prior experience in mindfulness or relaxation.

We offer in person training* or online training with dates to suit your needs.

Contact training@relaxkids.com or visit www.calmaclass.com to receive an information pack!

© Relax Ki
www.relaxki

* Minimum numbers apply.

RELAX KIDS CLASSES

Helping Children Shine

Join our magical, creative and fun classes especially designed to help your child become more resilient, calm and confident. Your child will receive a unique toolbox of relaxation and mindful exercises to help support their mental and emotional health and wellbeing.

THE 7 STEPS TO RELAXATION:

MOVE - warm up exercises for energy and fun

PLAY - mindful games for creativity and concentration

STRETCH - for balance and strength

FEEL - peer/self massage for self awareness, empathy and respect

BREATHE - for anxiety and inner calm

BELIEVE - for self esteem, confidence and positivity

RELAX - for imagination

HELP YOUR CHILD:

Relax and be calm
Feel confident
Focus and concentrate
Be imaginative
Develop creativity
Sleep better

WE HAVE OVER 5000 COACHES IN 48 COUNTRIES GLOBALLY. FIND A RELAX KIDS CLASS IN YOUR AREA VISIT WWW.RELAXKIDS.COM

OUR FRANCHISES:

Suitable for ages 3+.
Relax Kids classes are fun and creative, helping children become more resilient and improving their emotions. By giving children a toolbox of relaxation and mindfulness exercises from a young age, they will grow up with good mental health.

Suitable for ages 11+
ChargeUp sessions give young people mindful tools to help self-regulate. Sessions can help reduce stress and anxiety, improve sleep, mental health and wellbeing.

Suitable for ages 0-18 Months
Baby Mindful is a new approach to working with parents of young babies, and has been created to offer a range of activities which will stimulate and calm whilst supporting your baby's natural development.

FIND OUT MORE AT WWW.RELAXKIDS.COM

OUR STREET
BOOKS

Our Street Books for children of all ages, deliver a potent mix of
fantastic, rip-roaring adventure and fantasy stories to excite the
imagination; spiritual fiction to help the mind and the heart
grow; humorous stories to make the funny bone grow; historical
tales to evolve interest; and all manner of subjects that stretch
imagination, grab attention, inform, inspire and keep the pages
turning. Our subjects include Non-fiction and Fiction, Fantasy
and Science Fiction, Religious, Spiritual, Historical, Adventure,
Social Issues, Humour, Folk Tales and more.

Relax Kids Titles

Relax Kids: Aladdin's Magic Carpet

Let Snow White, the Wizard of Oz and other fairytale characters show you and your child how to meditate and relax.

Marneta Viegas

Using well-known and loved fairy stories this is a gentle and fun way of introducing children to the world of meditation and relaxation. It is designed to counteract some of the tensions with which we are all familiar at the end of a busy day, and offer parent and children, from3 upwards, together some quality time to relax and share. The meditations and visualisations aim to develop children's imagination and provide them with skills that will be invaluable for the rest of their life. Using 52 fairy stories and nursery rhymes like flying on Aladdin's magic carpet, climbing Jack's beanstalk, flying through the air like Peter Pan, swimming in the ocean with the Little Mermaid, asking a question of the Wizard of Oz, listening to the sounds of the forest with Snow White, and many others, children are encouraged to go on magical journeys in the mind.
Hardcover: December 4, 2003 978-1-90381-666-0 $14.95 £9.99.
Paperback: November 28, 2014, ISBN: 978-1-78279-869-9,
$14.95 £9.99

Relax Kids: The Magic Box

A book of 52 magical meditations to enhance your child's mental, emotional and physical wellbeing.

Marneta Viegas

The Magic Box is full of creative visualisations, meditations and relaxations. Children can imagine they are on a tropical island, flying into space, in a hot air balloon, time travelling, and leaving their worries on the worry tree. The book combines fantasy story meditations with deep relaxations, simple mindfulness exercises and positive affirmations. It is a great way to introduce meditation and mindfulness to young children. Practiced regularly, these exercises can have a profound effect on children's mental, emotional and physical wellbeing.
Paperback: March 28, 2014, 978-1-78279-187-4, $14.95 £9.99.

Relax Kids: The Wishing Star

Helping wishes and dreams come true with positive thinking, guided visualisations and affirmations for children.

Marneta Viegas

Using guided meditations based around traditional stories this is a gentle and fun way of introducing older children to the world of meditation and relaxation. It is designed to counteract some of the tensions with which we are all familiar at the end of a busy day, and offer parent and children together some quality time to relax and share. The meditations and visualisations aim to develop children's imagination and provide them with skills that will be invaluable for the rest of their life. For children aged 5 upwards.

Hardcover: January 20, 2005, 978-1-90381-677-6, $14.95 £9.99.
Paperback: November 28, 2014, ISBN: 978-1-78279-870-5, $14.95 £9.99.

Relax Kids: The Little Book of Stars

Helping children see their true star quality with simple visualisation exercises.
Marneta Viegas

The Little Book of Stars is the perfect way to introduce toddlers to relaxation and meditation. Each page explores a positive quality or value in an easy-to understand and child friendly way. Examples include Happy Star, Calm Star, Brilliant Star and Generous Star. This book is designed to engage very young children while introducing them to simple relaxation and mindfulness techniques. Each relaxation exercise takes around 3-5 mins. The exercises in the book also aim help develop children's sense of awareness and self-worth so promoting confidence and self-esteem. This book can be used at home, before nap time or bedtime or in nursery and kindergarten schools. Ages 2-5.

Paperback: November 28, 2014, ISBN: 978-1-78279-460-8,
Price: $14.95 £9.99.

Relax Kids: How to be Happy

Teaching children the true meaning of happiness and helping them create happy family moments at home.
52 positive activities for children
Marneta Viegas

How to be Happy is a scrap book bursting with positive ideas, simple and economical activities and fun games. Each page includes colourful pictures and diagrams to explain the activity in simple child-like language. There are some in-book activities but this is mainly a book of ideas. This book is full of interesting ways to relax, have fun and be happy. It encourages spirituality for young children. Each chapter is a different activity such as how to make peace pebbles, how to make a chill out corner, how to be kind, how to relax, how to manage stress, how to write a personal prayer, how to make worry dolls. The book is written in child language and so would be easily accessible to young families. It makes it easy for families to embrace simple spirituality, acts of kindness and spiritual activities. The book is designed to bring families together and allow children to enjoy spending quality time with their parents. It aims to help children manage their worries, anxiety and emotions whilst helping them grow up to be confident and happy. Ages 4-7.

Paperback: December 12, 2014, ISBN: 978-1-78279-162-1, $14.95 £9.99.

Relax Kids: Pants of Peace

Allowing children to enter the world of their imagination with positive thinking and visualisations.

52 meditation tools for children

Marneta Viegas

An innovative book that helps children get in touch with a wide range of inner qualities and values through creative meditation and affirmations exercises. Examples include shoe of confidence, cloak of protection, pen of appreciation and hat of happiness. Each meditation takes a positive quality or value and shows children in a creative and imaginative way how to develop that quality to improve their own life. This book encourages children to enjoy moments of calm and also helps develop their imaginations in a world of electronic gadgets. Pants of Peace is perfect for parents and teachers to read with children. The exercises are a toolkit to help develop children's mental health and well-being. Regular listening to these simple meditations can help children become more self-aware, positive and confident. This book can be used at home to help children relax or in the classroom. Ages 6+ The Relax Kids series is currently available worldwide.

Paperback: August 29, 2014, ISBN: 978-1-78279-199-7, $14.95 £9.99.

CD available at http://www.relaxkids.com/UK/Audio CDs

Relax Kids: Be Brilliant

52 pull-out affirmation games, cards and activities for children

(ages 4+)

Marneta Viegas

This book has been created to encourage children to be kind, loving and happy. It is a colourful book that bursts with fun and creativity. An ideal rainy day activity-book for families who want to instil positive values in their children, it provides parents and grandparents with an invaluable alternative to the monotonous worlds of gaming and apps. Activities include kindness tokens, IOU cards, positivity charts and affirmation dice, all of which Marneta Viegas uses innovatively in her ongoing mission to create an immersive, colourful and encouraging world for children, which will boost their esteem, confidence, and enjoyment of their surroundings. This book can be used at home or in the classroom to help children relax. Ages 6+. The Relax Kids series is available worldwide.

Paperback: December 12, 2014, ISBN: 978-1-78279-237-6, $14.95 £9.99